MAR 2 5 2003

EGGS

HARVEST TO HOME

Lynn M. Stone

Rourke Publishing LLC
Vero Beach, Florida 32964

www.rourkepublishing.com

PHOTO CREDITS:
All photos © Lynn M. Stone except p. 4 courtesy of Creighton Brothers Hatchery
and p.8 courtesy of American Egg Board

EDITORIAL SERVICES:
Pamela Schroeder

Library of Congress Cataloging-in-Publication Data

Stone, Lynn M.
    Eggs / Lynn M. Stone.
      p. cm. — (Harvest to home)
    ISBN 1-58952-126-9
    1. Eggs—Juvenile literature. [1. Eggs] I. Title

SF490.3 .S76 2001
635.5'142—dc21   2001031666

Printed in the USA

TABLE OF CONTENTS

EGGS

All birds lay eggs. But the only eggs most North Americans eat are from chickens, or **hens**. North Americans have a big taste for eggs! Farmers in the United States own about 275 million chickens. All these chickens do is lay eggs. These birds, called **layers**, make about 7 billion eggs each year. Most of those eggs are gobbled up by Americans.

Laying hens produce billions of eggs on American egg farms.

Female chickens and other birds make eggs in their bodies. The bird lays the egg when it is ready in its hard shell.

Chickens don't lay eggs because people love to eat them. An egg is what holds a bird's baby. Birds lay eggs to make more birds!

When you crack open an egg from the store, you don't find a chick. You find a yellow **yolk** and clear, watery liquid, called the egg "white." Why isn't there a chick?

A chick hatches from a fertilized egg. Some chicks grow up to be layers.

An egg has a baby in it only if it is **fertile**. For any female bird to make a fertile egg, she must mate with a male. However, hens will lay eggs if they mate with **roosters** or not. Egg farmers keep their hens away from roosters—the farmers do not want fertile eggs. Nearly all eggs sold for food in North America are **infertile**. They do not have chicks in them.

Both egg yolk and white have many **nutrients**, called protein, calcium, and vitamins. Nutrients are good for people.

Eggs make tasty dishes, like these scrambled eggs.

CHICKENS

Hens on **commercial** egg farms begin laying eggs when they are about 5 months old. They keep laying eggs for about 2 years. "Good" hens lay about 250 eggs each year.

Most layers in the United States are white leghorns. They are small, but they grow quickly and lay many eggs.

White leghorns lay white-shelled eggs. Some other kinds of chickens lay brown-shelled eggs. They are popular in New England.

Hens used as layers begin egg laying when they're about 5 months old.

11

Hens on small farms still lay eggs in nest boxes or in loose straw.

Workers in the packing room start eggs on their journey from chicken to egg carton.

EGG FARMS

Many big egg farms are owned by large companies. Each company may own many farms and buildings in different places. Almost 300 egg companies in the United States have more than 75,000 layers each. About 60 of these companies have more than 1 million hens each. Ten companies have more than 5 million layers each!

Egg-laying chickens live in this laying house in Indiana.

Chickens on the big farms live indoors in long buildings called laying houses. Some lay their eggs in cages. Others live in floor pens.

Having hens indoors helps farmers keep them healthy and laying eggs. Farmers can control the heat and light indoors. Chickens lay more eggs when it is light. By keeping lights on indoors, farmers keep hens laying more eggs all year around.

Egg farms raise chicks that will grow up to be layers.

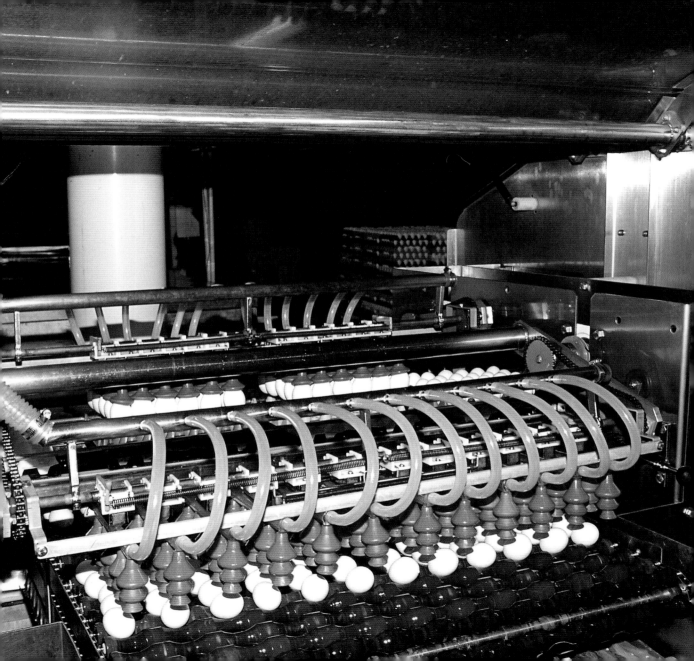

Indoor housing keeps foxes, hawks, and weasels from stealing hens. It also allows the farmer to control what the hens eat. Healthy, well-fed hens lay more eggs.

On today's egg farms, hens eat from feeders run by computers. Computers help plan the hens' food. Hens eat meal made mostly of corn, soybeans, vitamins, and minerals.

Eggs go to a packing area for washing, sorting, grading, and packing.

Hens on commercial farms lay eggs in special "nests" or onto a **sloping** floor. No one has to pick up the eggs. They roll onto a moving belt or into a chute.

The eggs go from the laying house to a packing room. Machines wash the eggs and move them to other work stations. One handler holds eggs against a light to check for tiny cracks or other problems.

Along the egg line, a worker checks eggs for quality.

Machines weigh eggs, sort them, and gently place them in cartons. Workers set the egg cartons in large boxes. Trucks with cold, **refrigerated** walls take eggs to stores. Eggs stay fresh when they are kept cool.

GLOSSARY

commercial (ke MUR shel) — a business that sells products to make money

fertile (FUR tel) — able to have babies

hen (HEN) — the female of some kinds of birds, such as chickens

infertile (in FUR tel) — unable to have babies

layer (LAY er) — a chicken used for egg-laying

nutrient (NOO tree ent) — healthy food or a healthy part of food, such as a vitamin

refrigerated (rih FRIJ eh ray ted) — to stay cold with electricity or ice

rooster (ROOS ter) — a male chicken

sloping (SLOHP ing) — slanting at an angle

yolk (YOHK) — the yellow part of an egg, where most of the nutrients are

INDEX

Further Reading

Stone, Lynn M. *Chickens*. Rourke Publishing, 1990

Websites To Visit

www.aeb.org (American Egg Board)

About The Author

Lynn Stone is the author of more than 400 children's books. He is a talented natural history photographer as well. Lynn, a former teacher, travels worldwide to photograph wildlife in its natural habitat.